T0064308

TIME TO
FORGIVE
AND FORGET

My Seven Day Spa Retreat

BRENDA KELLEHER-FLIGHT

BALBOA

PRESS

A DIVISION OF HAY HOUSE

Balboa Press books may be ordered through booksellers or by contacting:

Balboa Press
A Division of Hay House
1663 Liberty Drive
Bloomington, IN 47403
www.balboapress.com
1 (877) 407-4847

Because of the dynamic nature of the Internet, any web addresses or
links contained in this book may have changed since publication and
may no longer be valid. The views expressed in this work are solely those
of the author and do not necessarily reflect the views of the publisher,
and the publisher hereby disclaims any responsibility for them.

The author of this book does not dispense medical advice or prescribe the use
of any technique as a form of treatment for physical, emotional, or medical
problems without the advice of a physician, either directly or indirectly. The
intent of the author is only to offer information of a general nature to help
you in your quest for emotional and spiritual well-being. In the event you use
any of the information in this book for yourself, which is your constitutional
right, the author and the publisher assume no responsibility for your actions.

Any people depicted in stock imagery provided by Thinkstock are
models, and such images are being used for illustrative purposes only.
Certain stock imagery © Thinkstock.

Print information available on the last page.

ISBN: 978-1-5043-7999-1 (sc)
ISBN: 978-1-5043-8000-3 (e)

Balboa Press rev. date: 08/15/2017

Table of Contents

Introduction

I don't think of myself as an author and did not intend to write a self-help novel. I was challenged by a professor to write about the topic of time. For me, time is a mysterious concept. Sometimes it goes so fast, I can't account for its passing. Other times, it passes so slow I feel lost and anxious. Years and memories blend and I seem to have difficulty keeping track of exactly what happened when; I'm never sure whether what I remember is fact or fiction.

Working as a manager and a coach taught me that most of us experience difficult as well as joyful times as we journey through life. Many of our stories are very similar.

If this is true, why do so many of us feel as if we are alone and that no one else could ever understand our fears or worries? Why do we pretend to be happy when we are not or simply go along to get along?

I don't know the answers but I am sharing with you the free thoughts that came to my mind when I was pondering the topic of 'time.' I realized that sometimes we remember distant circumstances easier than we do recent events. To tell the truth, I also came to the conclusion that time could be whatever I wanted it to be. It could go fast or slow. I could see it as my friend or my enemy.

Even though I was not able to answer the question, "What is time?," I kept thinking about how our minds work, and how they can hold us hostage if we do not have the tools to master them.

The only thing I really know is that I have a choice; my mind can rule me or I can rule my mind. I choose to rule my mind. You can do that too.

I hope you identify with certain parts of this fictional journey. Please remember that the characters are not real. The story is intended to help each of us claim the life we deserve.

Most chapters outline tools you can use if you face situations similar to those encountered by the clients at the spa. As well, there are questions to ponder and ideas to assist you on your journey. If the tools intrigue you, please try them. Different techniques work for different people.

This book is meant to be your silent partner. I know I am grateful for the many authors who have helped me over the years and I hope this book will serve you well as you find the life you deserve.

Please take advantage of all the help this universe has to offer. You have a right to it.

Chapter 1

THE EXCITEMENT OF ANTICIPATION

I've always wanted to visit a spa for seven days. I like to go for a massage or a facial but I always leave wanting more. Right now, I need time to think and what better place to do it than in a spa. I chose a spa in Thailand because it was far from home, it sounded intriguing and I wanted to be alone. I wanted to relax and be silent.

My life was hectic. You know – husband, children, a job – and never enough hours in the day. I'm a coach. I work with teams, senior managers and individuals who are in conflict or trying to find harmony in their life and work.

Sometimes I'm asked what I know. I can't really answer that question because I've gathered knowledge and experience over many years and it seems to merge to one body of knowledge. To break it into tiny pieces appears impossible. Sometimes I absorb others' energy and that isn't always healthy for me.

I needed to get away and think, process, and let go. For weeks, I hunted for the perfect place. As soon as I found it, I immediately started packing my bags.

Of course, I'd need different outfits for different days. I thought I could not be seen in the same outfit on more than one day. I'd need books and my iPod. I'd want music for sure. When I stepped back and looked at my suitcase, I realized this was not what I wanted at all. I pulled everything out and started over.

Three bathing suits were enough. I could rinse them each night. All I needed was a couple of wraps in order to feel covered and comfortable walking from my room to the spa for my treatments. A couple of dresses would serve well if I chose to go to the dining room. I wasn't going to speak to anyone, anyway. This was to be a silent retreat. With those changes, the suitcase was half empty and I felt satisfied.

I checked with my boss to ensure there wasn't any trouble having the week off. I made sure all bills were paid and wrote my friends to let them know I'd be away for a week. My family would be just fine in my absence.

As I left my husband at the airport, I was a little nervous. After all, we always did things together. The questions and doubts started flooding my mind. Could I do this? Could I remain silent for seven days? Would I get tired of the spa treatments? What if I didn't like the spa? What if the service didn't live up to my expectations?

I stood in the check-in line and listened to all the chatter. I knew this was the best thing I could do right now. I needed this time. Slowly, as I talked myself through the doubt, the excitement returned and I began to relax.

When my flight was called, I could feel an overwhelming sense of satisfaction. I was doing something for me. Something that would help me connect deeply with myself. I had no idea what all this meant. I was going somewhere for a new experience. I might return the same person or I might change. The unknowns made me feel exhilarated. This was my adventure.

As the plane landed, I recognized I had to embrace the unknown. I also knew that it was easy for me to be discouraged and question my choices. This was for real. I was no longer talking about it. I had taken action and now my wish was becoming a reality.

I came down the steps of the arrivals floor and there was a man holding a sign with my name on it. What a relief. I picked up my bags and the kind man took them to the car. The taxi ride to the spa was uneventful. I didn't understand the language which suited me just fine. This was my dream – a silent spa retreat.

As we pulled up to the spa, I took a deep breath. The buildings were built of the most beautiful dark wood. I couldn't wait to touch it and feel close to nature. The flowers were in full bloom, almost as if they were inviting me into their world with ease and grace. The vivid reds, oranges and yellows were perfect. Each blossom welcomed me with a fragrance that relaxed me.

My mind started racing. I noticed the chairs and tables outside and thought, "What a place to sit and watch the ocean." Then I noticed a bar with beautiful wooden stools with green velvet seats. I bet there would be lots of healthy drinks there to soothe my soul and quench my thirst. As I turned, I heard exquisite music. It was soft and flowing. It washed over my tired body and mind, and I immediately felt peaceful.

I walked a few feet to open the door to the main desk but all I could see was an incredible blue-green ocean, silky sand and large wooden lounging chairs with emerald green cushions.

"This is my place. I am going to love it here."

I entered and signed in. Now my concern moved to the quality of the room. Would it be small and dingy? Would it be large and bright? Would I feel like a trapped animal after a day or two or would I love having my own private space to enjoy my own company?

The kind receptionist interrupted my thoughts as she welcomed me and outlined what was included in my package:

Day 1 - A facial and full body massage.
Day 2 - A pedicure and manicure along with a hand and foot massage, as well as a hair washing and styling
Day 3 - A toxin reducing body wrap and hot rock massage.
Day 4 - A back, face and neck massage.
Day 5 - An exfoliation massage.
Day 6 - An aromatherapy massage, scalp massage and hair treatment and styling.
Day 7 - A full relaxation body massage and another treatment of my choice.

She explained that I could change the treatments if the schedule did not meet my expectations. I didn't see much to complain about. I thanked her and could feel myself smiling from ear to ear. I accepted the key and headed to my room.

By this time, my imagination was running wild. I was imagining a week without having to speak to anyone. As I turned the key, I realized I was holding my breath. This next part was really, really important. I slowly opened the door and could feel every bit of tension leave my body.

The room was big. There was a queen- size bed with a beautiful white cotton duvet and four large pillows. One of the walls was comprised of built-in book shelves. Some of the shelves were removed to make room for an apartment-size refrigerator. There was a beautiful red and white carpet on a rugged wooden floor.

To the right of the bed was a small round walnut table with two chairs and close by was a rocking chair. I find rocking soothing. I twirled and twirled, flinging my arms in the air. I loved this space.

Quickly I moved to the window. Just as I had imagined, it was overlooking the ocean. I opened the window to hear the waves. Just like the relaxing scents of the flowers, the ocean's soothing colours also welcomed me. This was my dream. This is going to be the best time of my life – Silent, Relaxing, and Rejuvenating.

Chapter 2

ALONE IN A CROWD

I woke up pinching myself. I couldn't believe I was free to enjoy seven beautiful days pampering myself. I did not have to speak with one person. All I needed to do was bask in the sun, swim, eat good food and enjoy my treatments. What a life!

I stretched and realized that this was the perfect trip. I felt like a five year old who was totally excited about the adventures ahead of me. My first appointment wasn't until 11a.m., therefore, I could take my time.

I wondered how many people felt like their lives were based on their boss's, their spouse's, their children's or their family's needs, wants, and expectations. Maybe I am the only one who feels that way. I'm sure that the other ladies at this spa live and have lived a very privileged life.

One thing I was sure of was that I would have nothing in common with them. They probably come to a spa every few months or at least once a year. This is a once-in-a-lifetime trip for me.

I walked into the shower and just let the hot water cascade over my head and down my body. I'm not even sure how long I stayed in there. I could feel all the stress of life wash away. As I rolled my head from side to side, I could feel the tension release. This is just what I needed or as my mother would say, "Just what the doctor ordered."

What to wear? It doesn't matter really, does it? I don't know anyone and they don't know me. There won't be any conversations, therefore, there won't be a need to impress anyone.

I glided down the beautiful wooden stair case feeling the warmth of the wood under my hand. Music was playing softly. It felt so serene. The cushions on the chairs below were beautiful pastel patterns of pinks, greens, and blues. The vividness of the colors seemed to engulf me and make me feel very alive.

The dining room was loud. The women were talking incessantly. Their voices were animated as if they were competing with each other. I pointed to the name tag I was wearing which indicated I was on a silent retreat. The kind hostess led me to a table by the window. As I sipped my coffee and ate a juicy fresh orange, I looked out at the ocean and told myself to ignore the voices beside me. The orange sprayed its nectar over me as I started to peel it.

At home, the oranges are sometimes dry by the time they reach my supermarket. Here the orange was fresh, juicy, and sweet. I savored each section as if I were eating caviar. The smell of the coffee floated past my nose. It was perfectly brewed. To me, there is nothing like a good cup of coffee first thing in the morning. I put my hands around the cup, cradled it in my hands to feel the warmth, and slowly sipped it with great delight.

As I sat there, my mind kept thinking about all the times I spent talking and missing all the sights, sounds and feelings around me. I realized I have been numb to the world around me much of the time. I always blamed it on the fact that I was busy.

But why was I so busy? Where was I going? What was it all about anyway?

Was I really busy? Was I running from my inner thoughts? Was I fulfilled or did I feel as if there should be more to life? Was I in touch with myself or was I busy living the life others expected me to live in order to meet their needs? This line of thought was too heavy for me right now. I pushed the thoughts aside and went back to finish my perfect breakfast.

Feeling full and satisfied, I left for my facial and full body massage. There was a bounce in my step as I walked down the hall to the spa. I opened the door and presented my card. It was clear they knew I was on a silent retreat and were prepared for me. Without a word being spoken, I was led to a beautiful warm change room.

The shelves were made of mahogany. There was sage incense burning and the music was soft classical guitar. Sunlight shone gently though the half-glazed window. I stood in the sun and let the warmth fill my body and mind. Upon entering the room for the facial, I realized there were three chairs. I prayed the other two were empty. I hadn't finished my thoughts when two very boisterous women arrived and sat next to me.

All I hoped was that the therapist would put clay masks on their faces and they wouldn't be able to speak. Wrong!

Well, I soon learned that one lady was named Cheryl and her friend was Betty. I tried to tune them out but couldn't.

"Cheryl, John is such an inconsiderate guy."

"Why?"

"I got all dressed up to go to Henry's party. I looked and felt fabulous. We went there and John gave me a drink. Then he left to talk to his buddies. He's a real socialite. I didn't see him again until it was time to go home."

"What's wrong with that?"

"I feel he should stay with me. Look after me. I'm his date. Don't you agree with me?"

"Well Betty, what are you doing while he's socializing?"

"What do you think Cheryl? I'm getting drunker and madder by the minute."

"Could you go and talk to some other people?"

"Don't be a dork, Cheryl. All the others know each other. They are standing around in little groups just talking and laughing. The truth is they are mainly competing with each other."

"I don't understand what you mean by competing."

"You know Cheryl, if one says they visited Thailand, another says 'Oh! We went to Thailand and China.' It's all one-upmanship. I hate it. There is no depth to their conversations. It's all superficial and unconnected."

"What would you like to talk about, Betty?"

"Things that are meaningful. I'd like to hear their stories. What makes them happy and what makes them sad. I'd like them to be real."

"Come on, Betty. No one is going to tell you their stories in the middle of a party."

"Well then, couldn't they share what they learned about the culture in another country? How did their visit impact them? Did it cause them to re-evaluate their own thoughts, beliefs and things they take for granted at home? Is that too much to ask?"

"What could you do to shift the conversation and make it more meaningful?"

"Betty, are you trying to play shrink?"

"Not really."

By the time the banter finished, I was exhausted and just wanted to leave and go to my room.

I lay on my bed and replayed their conversation over and over again. I was mad at myself for giving Betty and Cheryl any of my attention. I was also beginning to think about myself in similar situations and wondered what I would do.

I knew getting drunk or mad wasn't a solution to Betty's concerns. I also knew what it was like to enter a room and feel left out or neglected. As I thought about it, I realized how awful I felt during those occasions. I felt unimportant, abandoned, and alone. The feelings started to overwhelm me.

To deal with them, I sat with a piece of paper and wrote out what I could do in a similar situation. It always helps me to write my thoughts.

If I Were Betty What Could I Do

I could look around the room to find another person standing alone. I could approach them and begin my own conversation. I would use the formula 'SWOT' to keep the conversation going. This is a formula I re-developed to help myself overcome my shyness and to help my clients who hate networking.

SWOT is a term I use when I plan for my own work and an easy one to use to generate good open-ended questions to keep a conversation moving and build harmony. The S = Strengths; W = Weakness; O = Opportunities; and T = Threats.

- ✓ Strengths (I would look for connections) – "Hello, my name is Katherine and your name is…? What brings you to this wonderful party?"
  - o Here is where I find out who they know and why they were invited.
- ✓ Weaknesses (I am looking for concerns) – I would ask, "Do you know most people here or are you new to the group?"
  - o This is the point at which people tell me their concerns such as:
    - ▪ "I don't know a soul here."
    - ▪ "I hate large groups; I prefer small intimate gatherings."

- ▪ "I'm really shy."
- ✓ Opportunities (I am trying to find out the benefits of attending the party) – I ask, "Are there people you would like to meet or information you would like to glean at this party?"
  - o Individuals may respond with:
    - ▪ "I want to meet such and such a person because I would like to work with their company."
    - ▪ "I am trying to find someone with whom I can share driving to and from school."
    - ▪ "I am trying to find a bridge club or book club to join."
    - ▪ "I'm new and would just like to have the opportunity to really connect with people in this town."
- ✓ Threats (I want to see if I can help them with their concerns) – I ask, "Are parties one of your favourite ways of meeting new people?"
  - o At this point, people may tell me their main concerns such as:
    - ▪ "I hate staying out late and these parties just go on and on. I'm always told that we have to stay because it is important to stay on the host's good side."
    - ▪ "John's ex-wife/girlfriend is also here and that makes me uncomfortable."
    - ▪ "Bill is thinking of moving his business and I'm trying to win him back and convince him to stay with us."

My mind still couldn't relax.

Questions for Betty to Consider

Could I and my partner talk about the party before we go and set mutual parameters?

Could I ask my partner to introduce me to at least two people when we arrive and make sure I am engaged in conversation before he leaves me to join his buddies?

Could my partner make a point of checking with me every hour or so to make sure I am feeling okay in this situation?

Could my partner invite me to join some of his conversations and at the same time provide me with an opportunity to expand my network?

Is there a way for me to find out who will be at the party and use social media to learn details that would help as conversation starters?

Could I ask the hostess to introduce me to at least one person before leaving me on my own?

Could the hostess watch for persons who are standing alone, approach them, and provide an opportunity for them to mingle?

Could I offer to help the hostess? If I am helping I would naturally have a reason to stop and talk to the other guests.

Could my partner and I agree on a time to leave so that I won't feel in limbo all night?

At this point, I must have been totally exhausted. I honestly don't remember falling asleep. I awoke just in time to leave for my full body massage. I prayed that I would be alone for this experience. My anxiety level was rising as I approached the spa. I silently prayed, "Please, God, let me be alone!"

Luckily, a very kind massage therapist named Marie led me to a private oasis. The music was soft and therapeutic. The sheets were warm. I could barely hear Marie move around the room as she prepared the lotions for my massage. What a gift. The gift of peace and quiet.

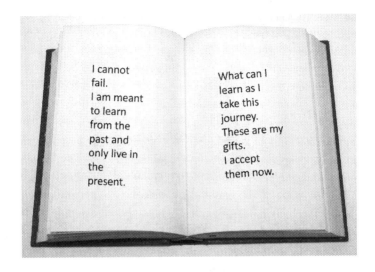

I cannot fail.
I am meant to learn from the past and only live in the present.

What can I learn as I take this journey.
These are my gifts.
I accept them now.

Chapter 2: **Lessons and Questions to Ponder**

Lesson 1: Every situation cannot be about me. I cannot be the center of attention. I need to know and share my truth with loved ones.

Questions: What do I need to feel safe?

Have I told my partner what I need in order to feel comfortable and safe or am I expecting him to intuitively know it?

Lesson 2: Confidence is every person's right.

Question: What does confidence look like, sound like and feel like to me?

Lesson 3: Networking skills can be learned. It's about pulling others towards ourselves.

Question: When do I feel uncomfortable? What networking skills do I need to learn to deal with my own discomfort?

Today's Gift for Me

There was a point in my life when I was very selfish. I didn't know it then but I could only see things from my point of view. I was afraid to ask for what I wanted from another person. Fear of being isolated terrified me.

I no longer feel that way because I've taken the time to learn networking skills (which everyone can learn, by the way). Maybe that's why I feel good when a client shares her success stories after our coaching sessions.

It's taken me a long time but now I speak my truth and ask for help and clarification of situations when I need it.

Thank you, Universe.

Chapter 3

BETRAYAL

This is Day 2. I love getting a pedicure and manicure. Getting a head massage and my hair groomed has always been my favourite things to do when I feel tired or down. Today had to be different. I needed peace and time to contemplate my present and my future. I needed a clear vision.

When I say a clear vision, I mean really being able to feel, see and hear what I want for myself. I call it "making a reel." It's like making a movie, ensuring that each detail is what I really intend.

As my mind started to develop my story, I decided to soak in the bath before going to the spa. The retreat had lavender Epsom salts on the shelf over the bath. I poured about two cups of it in the tub and turned on the hot water filling the tub to the top. As I sat in the tub for 30 minutes, the feeling of bliss returned and the tiredness vanished.

I think I was tired because I was unable to ignore the conversations around me. I was playing coach in my mind. Don't get me wrong, I love coaching. I love the success others achieve. The letters and emails I receive from clients leave me feeling very motivated to continue this work. Unfortunately, I didn't come here as a coach. I came as a very curious person who was on a focused journey to relax and rejuvenate.

I slowly climbed out of the tub, put on a cozy cotton wrap and proceeded to get dressed for breakfast. This morning I decided to have breakfast in the quiet comfort of my room. The orange was fresh and the coffee was perfect.

As I sipped my coffee, I remembered waking up each morning to the smell of fresh coffee being brewed on a wood stove. That smell meant it was going to be a great day. That's the only real memory I have of my father. All of a sudden I was feeling nostalgic. This had to stop. Slowly I moved my attention to the large juicy orange. As a child, my mother tried to get me to eat eggs and cream of wheat. I hated both. Even now, I really don't enjoy breakfast. An orange is about the most I can eat with a positive frame of mind.

As I left my room, I noticed a beautiful painting. It was a watercolour of two people dancing. I felt like raising my arms and flying down the staircase to the spa. Dancing is such a freeing experience. Our bodies flow to the music and all the troubles of the world vanish. My thoughts came to a halt as I approached the spa.

Inside it appeared to be quiet. I knew this was going to be a wonderful experience. That thought vanished as soon as I heard other ladies enter the room for their manicure and pedicure. I willed myself to ignore them and focus on the beauty of my own treatments. That did not work. I kept listening to their stories.

Ruby, the lady two chairs to the right of me, was telling her sister Judy about all of her regrets from childhood. Judy was trying to guarantee her stories were better and juicier than Ruby's.

"Judy, do you remember our childhood very well?"

"Naturally, Ruby, don't you?"

"I mean all the bad things that happened to us."

"How could I ever forget, Ruby?"

"Do you remember the time we were behind the house and the neighbour's kids convinced us to take three cigarettes from our father's package?"

"You didn't want to do it, Ruby. They badgered you and bullying you until you agreed to do it."

"You know Judy, I still feel guilty about that. I shouldn't have done it. I wanted them to like me and I thought the only way they would like me is if I did what they wanted."

"I know. You were only seven. What do you expect? We all do stupid things when we are young."

"But do we all regret those things in our adulthood, Judy?"

"I think the dumb things we do in our childhood always haunt us in our adulthood."

"Well, what's one thing you remember from our childhood?"

"I remember telling our oldest sister a true story of something that happened to me. She went to mom and said it was a lie and I was making it up. She laughed at me, made fun of me, and said that my imagination was running away with me."

"What did you do, Judy?"

"I went to my room, covered up in the bed clothes and cried until I fell asleep. I never trusted Joan after that. I felt really bad about myself and thought I was to blame. I hated myself to the point I wanted to change my name."

"Why change your name?"

"I thought that if I created a new identity things would be better. I thought our family would trust me and believe me. I thought I would be loved. Ruby, all I wanted was to be loved for who I was."

"Didn't you feel loved?"

"No, did you?"

"Not really. I was always seeking someone's approval. I think I lost myself somewhere back there."

"I think that is why I never feel happy. It's as if I'm waiting for the next shoe to drop all the time."

"I think I go from contentment to depression. I never really have ten good months in a row."

"Ruby, this conversation is depressing me. Can we pick it up when we are alone – later maybe?"

"For sure. Sorry for bringing your mood down."

"You didn't bring it down. That's why I'm here – to bring it up."

As I listened to that conversation, it was like déjà vu. I remember feeling very unloved. I thought I must have been adopted. These people couldn't be my real parents. If I were their child, I would automatically be loved. They would want to celebrate my gifts, teach me when I made mistakes, and mentor me as I pass through the ages and stages of childhood.

The truth is I didn't feel loved. I was punished when I made a mistake. I was never mentored. I didn't think I had any gifts. I felt as if I was in the way, a burden to be endured. I never really recovered from that feeling.

It hit me. I am exactly the same as Ruby and Judy. I feel just like they do. Maybe we had different experiences but the results were the same. The deep sadness was overwhelming. I wanted to cry but I couldn't. There were no tears – the sadness was too painful.

Here I was with Hollywood fingernails and toenails. My hair was done to perfection, and yet, I felt like an invisible, unwanted and unloved creature.

As I entered my room, I couldn't remember if I thanked the staff. I didn't hear the soft corridor music. I was like a zombie. I had no idea how I was going to deal with this situation. If I didn't do something, my perfect holiday would be ruined.

I sat in the large lounging chair, turned on my iPod. Eventually, my energy returned and I realized I needed to deal with this situation.

I took out a sheet of lined paper and drew a line down the center. I thought back to a time when I was 10 years old. The 10-year old in me needed to be heard. I am sharing my journal with you.

My Thoughts	Why
I don't feel loved by my family.	My mother and my sister stop talking when I come in the room
They should include me in the conversation.	I want to feel important.
I am alone and if they acknowledge me, I will feel better.	If they don't love me, why don't they give me away? Why ignore me?
They hate me	I'm not good enough, smart enough, independent enough, or pretty enough.
Why don't they tell me why they don't like me and let me change?	They don't care enough. I don't count.
If I counted, how would I know?	They would include me in conversations, play with me, take time to talk to me and wonder what I want or need. They would say "I love you."
I have evidence that they don't care.	I'm afraid of the dark and they send me to bed by myself. They didn't believe me when I said I had trouble with a teacher, or when I said my feet really hurt.

My Thoughts	Why
How did I let them know how much I was hurting?	I didn't. I was too afraid of being punished or ridiculed.
I kept silent.	Fear. I was constantly afraid.
Being afraid isn't helping	I feel too alone and isolated
I have no idea how to help myself	I have no tools, except hiding and crying
What can I do now that I'm grown up?	Sit with myself. Listen to myself. Show myself that I love me. Remember that if I cannot love me I cannot love another fully.
I have work to do	I need to release the feelings of sadness and isolation
I will use mindfulness practices while I am here at the spa. I can journal and every day I can arrange a treat for myself.	Because I am worth it. I am a good human being who deserves to let her light shine.

Writing this made me feel a little better. As with many of us, our memories of past events are not always accurate. We remember our house being bigger than it really was, we remember the sad times as being sadder and we remember our failures as if they were major catastrophes. In truth, everyone who raised us did the best they could at the time. The stories we create and the reactions we generate aren't always the most helpful. I'd like to show you tools that help me on a daily basis.

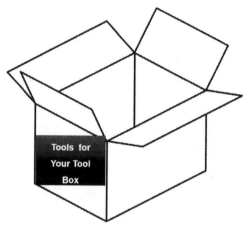

Tools for Your Tool Box

Prayer: *Talk to a power greater than yourself, especially if there is no other person you can trust.*

Meditation: *Sit quietly in a chair, making sure your feet are on the floor with palms facing down or up on your thighs. Listen to your thoughts as if you are an observer of them. Don't judge them or try and stop them. I find with this practice, my thoughts will subside and I find a place of peace.*

Pivoting: *Tell your story to yourself. When you are finished, tell it a different way by adding a different interpretation or ending. If it is negative, find at least three positives in it. For example, if being ignored made you feel sad and dejected, rewrite that part, and tell how experiencing that enables you to empathize with others, and be a really good listener and friend.*

Journaling: *Write in a journal. Tell your story as if you are telling it to your best friend. Find the lesson in each entry. When the journal is full, destroy it and move forward.*

Pounding: *Scan your body to find where you are holding a specific emotion. Then you can:*

- *Beat on a pillow*
- *Scream at the moon*
- *Run*
- *Punch a punching bag, or*
- *Bounce a ball until you are tired.*

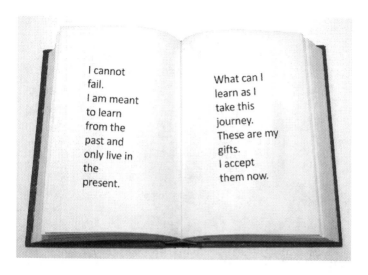

I cannot fail.
I am meant to learn from the past and only live in the present.

What can I learn as I take this journey.
These are my gifts.
I accept them now.

Chapter 3:   **Lessons and Questions to Ponder**

Lesson 1:   Peer pressure is real. It isn't something that happens in childhood only. Advertising, friends, family and social organizations tell us what to wear, how to speak, what is and is not acceptable, and what we need to do to get along.

Question: What do I do to get along while realizing that it is not based on what I truly believe or want?

Lesson 2:   Trust is the foundation for all relationships. Just because a person is a blood relative does not mean that s/he won't betray my trust. Trust is not just about being predictable. It is not about recrimination, abuse, or being rejected for thinking or feeling differently from someone else.

Question: Do I allow others to be vulnerable in my presence?

Today's Gift for Me

I realized that I didn't always trust myself. It took me quite some time to get in touch with my real self. Now the first person's opinion I trust is my own. I believe in myself. I know I still have lots of room for growth but I trust my intuition. That is a wonderful gift.

Chapter 4

HELPLESSNESS

It's Day 3. My head is spinning this morning. What did I do to deserve these interruptions? I came here to relax, unwind and contemplate.

I hoped the toxin-reducing body wrap and hot rock massage would take out the memories of my other unwelcome companions and leave me in a state of peace. I ran the bath, put on soft music and let my body float in the warm water. Gradually, I focused on each part of my body and could feel the tension in my legs, body, arms, hands, shoulders and face leave. What a gorgeous feeling. This is the heaven on earth I imagined.

I began to think about my spa experience back home. Each client has her own room. We don't share with others. I like that better. Why do I prefer that setup?

I think I like my privacy. I need time to process my own thoughts and let the world go away. My mood was becoming depressed. I needed to shake that feeling. I started repeating "today will be better" over and over.

A knock came on my door at 11am. I opened it to find my brunch. It consisted of fresh squeezed orange juice and an omelet made with peppers and onion. Slowly, I drank my juice and ate the omelet. Everything was above expectations. My compliments to the chef, I toasted silently.

I pulled on a magnificent rose-colored sheath dress I purchased in Paris. This dress fit like a glove. The V-neck and fine tailoring made me feel like a million dollars. I held on to this glorious emotion as I headed to the spa.

My vision of peace and tranquility soon vanished. The tables were only separated by free-standing room separators. Although I have to say the Japanese art on them was beautiful. I couldn't believe my luck. Well, maybe I would be the only person scheduled for the morning.

I lay on the table and the therapist began to massage my body. Oh! What a magnificent feeling. Soon I was drifting off into my own world. This was what I needed. I can't tell you where my mind went but it wasn't in the spa. I felt totally at peace.

All of a sudden my body jolted. There were loud voices. I could hear another therapist asking the ladies to be quiet – this was a quiet zone. I'm not sure if the other clients were selectively ignoring the message or were too arrogant to listen to the directions being provided.

My new-found cohabiters of the space were Georgie and Aimee. Clearly, they were close friends and were using this time as "girls' time." I couldn't ignore their conversation. I just settled in to listen. Is that rude? I'm not sure but I didn't have much choice. Oh, I should tell you that Aimee's voice was the squeakiest I'd ever heard. I was sure she could be heard for miles around.

"Georgie, I really want to deal with old family issues while I'm here."

"Why? What's going on?"

"I'm starting to have flashbacks of old memories."

"I'm a great listener but not much of a therapist, Aimee."

"When I was about seven or eight, my only uncle tried to have sexual intercourse with me!"

"Oh, my God, Aimee. Did he?"

"No. I kept pushing and pushing him away and he gave up."

"So if nothing happened, why are you thinking about it now?"

"You know, Georgie, I always felt violated. I never trusted him again. To this day I hate him. He should have apologized to me."

"Did you tell your mom?"

"Yes."

"What was her response?"

"She told me I was talking foolishness and to give it up."

"What did you say?"

"Nothing. I was too hurt. I never trusted her after that either."

"That's horrible."

"I know. How do I get past it?"

"You have a lot of emotions pushed down into your body, don't you?"

"Yes I do, Georgie, and I want you to help me let them go."

"What do you want me to do or say, Aimee?"

"I thought you were my friend and I could trust you to be there for me and help me."

"Hold on now, Aimee, I am your friend and I want to help. I just don't know how to help. Can I think about it?"

"What's there to think about? I just told you the story."

"If nothing really happened, why are you dealing with feelings of violation? You aren't feeling good about yourself."

"I think, in truth, Georgie, I really don't like myself."

"No one can make you hate yourself. That is your decision to make. You have chosen to hate yourself. It sounds as if you are blaming yourself for something that was beyond your control. Did you feel good about yourself before this happened?"

"I never thought about that before. No I didn't, not really."

"Were there other things that happened that made you feel bad about yourself?"

"No one ever told me they loved me, when I was little, I mean. I didn't have any friends. I was always alone, or that's how I felt. My grandparents raised me. I knew my mother but she lived in another town. When she remarried, I went to live with her and my stepdad."

"Was your stepdad nice?"

"Not really. He didn't care if I lived or died and my mom's main worry was keeping him happy."

"That's sad."

"I was too numb to know. I just went through the motions of living but I didn't feel connected to anyone or anything. It was when I was 19 that I made up my mind to make my own life. I had enough of their dysfunction."

"What did you do?"

"I left, got a job, and put myself through post-secondary school."

"Did you feel happy then?"

"I just focused on work and school. I wasn't happy or unhappy. I was too busy to be either. Being busy meant that I didn't really deal with my feelings either."

"Now is your time to listen to your body and let go of the past. You are my best friend and I love you for being there for me all the time. Let's pick up this conversation by the pool after we finish here. I'll consider your situation and see if I have any suggestions for you."

"You are the best. That's perfect."

When they left, I went for my hot rock treatment. My mind was racing. I remembered children who were taken from their families and put in residential schools only to be treated horribly. I reverted back to thinking as a coach. What could Aimee do to help with her situation? I reached for my journal and wrote until my hand and mind calmed.

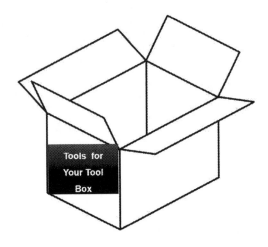

Tools for
Your Tool
Box

Journal: There a four ways to journal.

1. Write a topic on the top of a page. Write everything you feel about that topic. Then write everything you see when you think of that situation. Finally, write about each sound you hear and each smell that comes to mind.

2. Write an emotion on the top of a page. Stop, sit back and scan your body to find where you are holding that emotion. How does that body part feel? Do not try and think about it. Just let your hand write from the perspective of that body part. Let the release continue uncensored.

3. Write the title of a situation on the top of a page. Write as if you are the age at

which you experienced that situation. Next write from the perspective of the age you are now. Finally, write from the perspective of a good trusted friend. Compare the three versions, find the lessons, and determine whether you can use those lessons to move forward with your life.

4. Free write. Put your pen on a piece of paper and just write uncensored as thoughts and ideas come to your mind. Do not become distracted if the topics change constantly. Let your hand do the writing without judgement.

Visualize: Sit with your feet planted flatly on the floor. Put your hands, palms up, on your thighs. Close your eyes and imagine a vase of roses on a table in front of you. Imagine taking one of the roses and placing it in front of your third eye (slightly above and between your eyebrows. Slowly scan your body, starting with your toes. As you think of the situation at hand, let all of the negative feelings in your toes rise up your spine and face and enter the rose. When you finish with your toes, move to your feet and let all of the negative energy related to this particular situation rise up and enter the rose. Keep doing this with each part of the body. Don't forget your scalp, ears and throat. When you finish scanning each part of the body and you no longer feel energy entering the rose, visualize the rose breaking into a thousand pieces and returning to the universe with love and forgiveness.

Ask: Ask yourself why you interpret a story a specific way. Are there other ways to write it? Consider writing as follows:
- ➢ As yourself
- ➢ As the other person
- ➢ As a bystander
- ➢ As a person who learned many positive lessons that can be used to help others

Personal note: You may think there isn't anything to say, but be patient and try. I remember sitting with my sisters and brothers one time and recalling a certain happy situation all of us experienced. Each of us has written a different script about it. I was totally amazed. Ever since that day, it is much easier to re-write my stories.

Mindfulness: Sit quietly, close your eyes, and focus your awareness on the present moment. Deeply pay attention, calmly acknowledge and accept your feelings, thoughts, and bodily sensations. Let the feelings talk for themselves. Just sit and listen to what they have to say.

Take time each day to focus solely on the present.

Be fully aware of the 'now.' Savour each sound, smell, feeling, and the messages contained therein.

The key: No judgement!

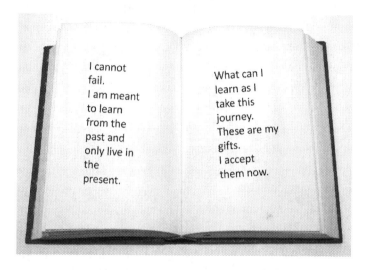

I cannot fail. I am meant to learn from the past and only live in the present.

What can I learn as I take this journey. These are my gifts. I accept them now.

Chapter 4:   Lessons and Questions to Ponder

Lesson 1:   Families have a responsibility to keep each other safe. Issues need to be discussed in an open and safe environment. Each child needs to know that her voice is heard. When voices are not heard, it can lead to feelings of rejection, abandonment, and low self-esteem.

Questions: Do I withhold judgement when another person tells me her story; am I empathetic?

What does empathy look like, sound like and feel like?

How can others tell when I am being empathetic?

Lesson 2:   Safety and belonging are two very basic human needs. If these needs are not met, it can have long-term negative consequences for the person involved.

Question: Knowing that there are times when I have not felt safe, what have I done with those emotions?

What tools can I use to release these unhealthy emotions in order to ensure they do not impact current relationships?

Today's Gift for Me

I grew up thinking that adults knew best. After many disappointments, I realized that what I was practicing was learned helplessness. That lesson hurt. Now I know there will be times when others will not please me, will intentionally hurt me, and/or be jealous of me. That is okay. I know that I have to search my own consciousness to make sure that I do not set unrealistic expectations for others. I do not need to judge others. I let them travel their own journey without drawing any conclusions. Peace be with you.

Chapter 5

HAUNTINGS FROM THE PAST

This was the half-way mark. It's Day 4 and the schedule says I'm having a back, face and neck massage. I was feeling very ambivalent. One part of me wanted this experience to never end. The other part of me wanted all these people to go away and take their miseries with them. Their stories were reminding me of my own garbage that is similar to so many others' stories. I am tired of my own willingness to let these stories control my reactions and feelings.

I decided to call the concierge to see if my massage could be scheduled at a time when the other clients were otherwise engaged. As soon as I asked, I felt guilty. Who am I to make such a selfish request? That thought soon vanished when she replied, "Sorry Madame, there are preferred clients who can book whenever they want."

I was so mad. My mind went on a field trip. Preferred clients! Who are preferred clients? Why aren't I a preferred client? There are class separations everywhere. What about equality? What about customer service? What about making each person feel special? Who are they anyway? I came here because of all the promises they made in their brochure. I am supposed to feel special. To feel relaxed and rejuvenated at the end of my stay. What a sucker for advertising!

By the time I finished my internal rant, I felt many old feelings I'd forgotten about. I remembered a time when I felt totally rejected and devastated. My friend told me she didn't invite me to a morning coffee because I was working and all her other friends were stay-at-home moms. I tried to calm myself by breathing deeply but my mind had no intention of cooperating.

Next, I remembered a time when I was 11 years old. We were all outside in the ball field at school. Team captains were chosen by the physical education teacher. These captains were asked to alternate choosing their team mates. I was the last person picked. I was new at the school and did not know a single person. I felt as if I wanted to die or run home or faint or something. Anything to get out of this situation. I held my head down for days after. It was totally humiliating.

Then there was the time my brother came into a gathering and spoke to everyone in the group except me. I could feel everyone's eyes on me. Their eyebrows told me what they were thinking, "What's going on here between the two of them?" In fact, I had no idea. My stomach muscles churned, my jaw pained and I wanted to run home as fast as my legs could carry me. Of course, I pretended not to notice. In truth, that situation really hurt me.

Suddenly, I realized how much hurt I held inside. Wow! How do I process this and let it go? I remembered something a coach asked me to do to show me how I was holding on to situations and ideas which were in the past. He was trying to show me that the past was gone forever. I did as he showed me. I put my hand in a glass of water that sat on my coffee table and tried to hold the water. Of course, I couldn't do that. That's like those memories; I couldn't bring them back, I needed to move on. The only question was, "How would I do that?"

A great idea struck me. When I am having my back, face and neck massage, I would set my intention to let that blocked negative energy leave.

I kept repeating my intention over and over again as I walked to the spa. A friendly receptionist opened the door as she saw me approaching. I was shown to my spa table and asked to remove all my clothing and lie under the sheet, facing downward.

As I lay there, I set my intention: I am going to let past hurts go with love.

As Margarete moved her hands gently up and down my spine and carefully rocked my body from left to right, I began to relax. I set my intention once more, closed my eyes, and gave thanks for this opportunity to really let go and move forward with my life.

I could feel myself drifting off to sleep just as Jo (I guess Josephine) and Debbie arrived. For the first 15 or so minutes there was glorious silence, then all hell broke loose.

"Debbie, do you remember all the fights mom and dad had when we were young?"

"I sure do, although I try not to think about them."

"I used to sit or lie in my bed and try to be very quiet. I was so scared."

"Deb, why didn't you tell me this before?"

"I didn't know if you felt the same way, Jo."

"I still have nightmares about those times."

"Go on. So do I."

"Deb, I've even seen a therapist to try and deal with my childhood issues. I hope you don't think I'm weak if I couldn't deal with them myself. Do you?"

"No. My body is a bag of knots. I've been uptight all my life and it's only now that I realize it was a result of hearing all that yelling, hitting, swearing, and threats. I've gone to massage therapy, had some energy work done, and ate a little too much trying to cope. You know, Jo, I'm glad we are talking now. I have so many health issues and I know they are related to my past."

"Did you know you were feeling stressed all those years?"

"No. did you?"

"No. I tried to bury those memories. I was coping but I wasn't releasing. I think I was only hurting myself."

"Jo, I know I was only hurting myself and it affected all of my relationships. I didn't really trust men. I kept all the negativity to myself. I never spoke my truth. In fact, I don't even know if I recognize my truth."

"Deb, you hit the nail on the head. I am so busy trying to be what my mother-in-law, my boss, my husband and my children expect of me. I don't really know who I am, what I think or what I want. That's scary isn't it?"

"What are we going to do, Jo?"

"I honestly don't know but we will figure it out."

At that point the conversation ended because the massage therapists asked them to turn over so that they could finish the treatments.

My therapist told me I was finished. I was to get dressed slowly and go to a meditation room, drink lots of water, and relax to enjoy the benefits of the treatment.

As I sat drinking the cool spring water, my thoughts quickly went back to Jo and Debbie. If they asked me to outline the signs of stress they should watch for within themselves, what would I say?"

Sauntering back to my room, I realized I was totally absorbed in thought. To get rid of them, I decided to open my journal and write. I'd like to share this part of my guide with you now.

Abrupt Demonstrations of Quick Temper

Quick temper is obvious when you deal with a person who shouts or uses profanities without apparent provocation. Her action may be the straw that put you over the edge. You display behaviour which is disproportionate to her action because you cannot subdue your tension levels any longer.

Action

1. Take note of the times and situations that aggravate you.
2. Note and acknowledge your personal triggers.
3. Understand exactly what you expect from another person.
4. Determine if there are other people who can act as a go-between and need to be present when you deal with specific individuals.
5. Refrain from judging the behavior, withdraw from the situation, and acknowledge that you will continue the conversation when you have had time to think about it.
6. Time your interactions to ensure that you have not been dealing with anything negative prior to meeting with someone who triggers you to have outbursts.

Blaming Others

Blaming others is a technique used when we do not want to face our own inadequacies. This deflection temporarily lowers our stress level. The unfortunate part of this situation is that the relief does not last long. Therefore, as the tension mounts, we need to find someone else to blame rather than dealing with our weaknesses.

Action

1. Ensure you understand exactly what others expect and meet those standards and deadlines.
2. Watch your behaviour and determine the circumstances under which you feel this need to find someone to blame, and avoid those situations.
3. Refrain from engaging in the blame game because if you are willing to blame others, you have to be willing to be the focus of the blame at some other time.
4. Ask for specifics when you are being blamed, and offer to take corrective action immediately. Make sure you follow through as expected.

Distractibility

We have a tendency to be distracted when we are focusing on issues that are playing over and over in our minds. These stories may or may not be accurate but we are attached to our versions. As a result, we are unable to focus on the here and now.

Action

1. Ask questions to ensure you are clear about what others want or what they are thinking.
2. Make eye contact and hold it while engaged in a conversation.
3. Note when we look away or our eyes glaze over, and ask a question to ensure we are listening and understanding.
4. Send an email or note outlining your understanding of the conversation, asking another to respond if there is any misunderstanding
5. Listen to another's concerns if s/he needs to vent let him/her do that: bring the conversation back to the situation at hand as soon as it is realistically possible.

Excessive Eating

Food appears to be such a good friend when there does not appear to be any other acceptable avenue to vent frustrations. This is particularly true in our culture, where many social activities revolve around food. There are advantages to using food as a friend. It does not talk back, judge, or criticize in any way. Unfortunately, there are also disadvantages to overeating. Fortunately, if you are overeating to deal with your stress, there are actions you can take.

Action

1. Listen actively to your own internal dialogue (concerns and issues).
2. Think of other ways to deal with the issues, list the pros and cons of each choice and choose the method that will serve you best.
3. Connect with professional or support groups.
4. Acknowledge your strengths.
5. Refrain from getting food as a reward or way to stay happy.

Failure to Take Breaks

If we are always busy, this can be an indication of high levels of stress. Over working, at home or on the job, can be a sign of avoidance. If we bury ourselves in tasks, we think we can avoid dealing with the difficulties that are troubling us. Unfortunately, overwork is only a temporary measure. Eventually, the issues will have to be dealt with in one way or another.

Action

1. Acknowledge when you appear to be unable to stop what you are doing, even for a short time, and wonder if there is anything you can do differently
2. Seek help.
3. Question yourself to see if you are avoiding another for any reason and if you need to apologize for anything.
4. Schedule breaks and follow through.
5. Join in the social aspects of home or work.

Fatigue

Fatigue is a result of stress. When we are stressed we do not sleep well and find it hard to relax. Fatigue will present as the inability to complete as much work/chores as expected, use of sick time, slowness in movement, or even falling asleep during the day.

Action

1. Wonder if the expectations of yourself are too high, if the work is meaningful, or if your roles are satisfying, and acknowledge your truth.
2. Take appropriate breaks and sufficient holidays.
3. Acknowledge that you are always tired and question what you can do to regain energy.
4. Schedule "me" times.

Focusing on Shortcomings

When we do not feel good about ourselves, we attempt to feel better by pointing out others' shortcomings. We make sure everyone sees others' weaknesses. When we point out these flaws, we temporarily feel better about ourselves. We fail to recognize that we are mirrors of each other. Things we like in others are reflections of our strengths. The things we do not like in others are mirrors of our own weaknesses that may be dormant or visible to others.

Action

1. Acknowledge that you are the best role model if you refrain from discussing others' personal characteristics and walk away from any such discussions; focus on issues and not people.
2. Note and recognize others' strengths when someone is pointing out his needs.
3. Do not partake in personality assassinations (including your own).

Manipulating Information

When we are stressed, we are often willing to take action, which we would not consider if our circumstances were different. Some of the behaviours you may note include:

- Insisting that our information be considered as the only necessary information
- Manipulating financials
- Overbilling or overspending
- Changing information to make things look more favourable than they are
- Telling only part of a story
- Changing our story as time goes by, and/or
- Refusing to let others, such as partners, see our records.

Manipulating Information

Action

1. Note comments or behaviours that indicate you are under considerable stress in a particular aspect of your life.

2. Ask yourself concrete open-ended questions that require openness and transparency; rigid thinking holds you back.

3. Ask for specifics from more than one source and compare information.

4. Ask yourself why you feel it necessary to be defensive or avoid presenting all options with the pros and cons for consideration and decision making.

5. Insist on gathering all the facts and making sound decisions.

Micromanaging Another

When we are stressed, common behaviours include micromanaging others. We ask details and intrusive questions, want others to account for their whereabouts all the time, wonder what others are discussing, and want to be involved in matters that really do not require our input. This pattern may be visible at home and at work.

Action

1. Clarify your expectations and be open to problem solving if the other person needs your help. Accept that asking for help is a sign of strength rather than a sign of weakness.
2. Ask others about their specific concerns and make sure they are addressed.
3. Always act respectful and inclusive.
4. Refrain from any avoidance behaviours,
5. Include the other persons in problem-solving efforts; do not discuss her issues behind her back.
6. Give other person credit where credit is due.

Poor Personal Appearance

It is difficult for us to be concerned about how we appear to others when we are focused on our own issues. The issues or stressors seem to be insurmountable and we can lose hope of resolution. Therefore, our internal thoughts say, "Why bother."

Action

1. Celebrate work well done (small achievements).
2. Say positive comments which focus on your strengths.
3. Take advantage of our own or community support services.
4. Note ways you can help yourself and take action.
5. Be honest about aspects of our personal appearance which are negatively impacting others.

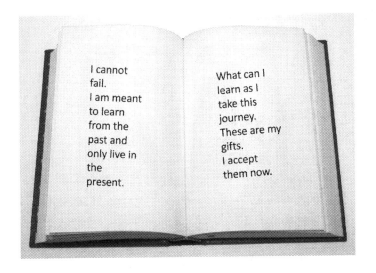

I cannot fail.
I am meant to learn from the past and only live in the present.

What can I learn as I take this journey. These are my gifts.
I accept them now.

Chapter 5: Lessons and Questions to Ponder

Lesson 1: I must choose between temporary discomfort and permanent resentment. If I let the little things pass, they will build and before I know it I may say or do something I will live to regret.

Question: Do I choose temporary discomfort over permanent resentment?

Lesson 2: We are mirrors of each other.

Question: Do I acknowledge that the things I like about another person are things I like about myself, and the things I dislike about that person are the things I still need to resolve or deal with for my own benefit?

Lesson 3: Rejection is painful. My thoughts are telling me that no cares about me. I feel invisible, unworthy, and less than others. The pain can be long lasting.

When a person rejects me with her actions, it hurts just as much as when she uses words.

Questions: How have I coped when have I been rejected?

What is really happening when a person rejects someone else? Does it say more about the rejecter or the rejected?

Lesson 4: Hearing a negative situation can be as negative for a child as if she had witnessed it visually. Unresolved emotions become buried and have long-lasting damaging effects.

Questions: What negative situations have affected me in a traumatic way? Can I list them?

Today's Gift for Me

I've been rejected, snubbed, and hurt. I know I can be bossy, too direct, and overbearing. Thank goodness I've been able to look at my past as a story, accept that my memories may not be totally accurate, and realize that the past is gone.

I have chosen how I interpret the past, deciphered the lessons, and use that information to deal with all the wonderful "presents" the universe hands me each day.

It is important to connect with others on a personal level and deposit in each other's emotional bank account. I cannot withdraw what I haven't deposited.

We are mirrors of each other and in order to love you, I have to love myself first.

I know we were all born perfect. You are perfect. Do not let your story hold you back. Namaste!

Chapter 6

BURIED ALIVE

The sun is shining through my windows as I awake to a beautiful new day. The experiences at this retreat are leaving me feeling exhausted. I am learning about myself. I'm also learning that many women here have similar stories.

This was not my intent for this holiday. I worked hard to save the money to come here. All I wanted was to relax and release all the old worn out memories I was carrying in my physical and energy bodies. Is that so much to ask? Pondering that question made me realize that I am releasing the power of those old useless memories. I am taking the lessons and moving forward!

My energy level was very low. My legs felt heavy and my face felt as if it was frozen in a frown. I filled my bath and decided to play rock and roll music to lift my spirits. I spent time sitting in the warm water. Finally, it hit me like a ton of bricks. I could sit and feel miserable or I could express gratitude for the gifts in my life. I didn't care that my hands were wet. I reached for my pencil and journal. I can't offer suggestions to my clients if I don't follow them myself. The pencil moved gracefully and effortlessly on the page.

Gratitude

Things for which I am grateful:

- ✓ The ability to see
- ✓ The ability to walk
- ✓ The money that made it possible for me to come here
- ✓ The beautiful food
- ✓ The patient massage therapists
- ✓ The airlines that brought me here
- ✓ The sun, moon and stars
- ✓ The ability to hear the water move on the sand
- ✓ My husband
- ✓ My children
- ✓ My grandchildren
- ✓ The ability to read
- ✓ The freedom I experience in my country
- ✓ The ability to choose what I want and need
- ✓ The ability to paint
- ✓ The ability to coach others and see positive changes in their lives...

It seemed as if there was so much abundance in my life. I could have kept on writing forever, or that's how it seemed.

At least my mood was lifting and I was ready for my exfoliating massage. All I wanted was to slough off the old and breathe in the new. Today was a new beginning. The past is gone and this is my present.

As I entered the spa, all I could hear was laughter. I learned that the other cubicles were filled with a bridal party. This was their stagette getaway. Oh joy! I sound like a Grinch, don't I? I really don't mean to, but this is too much. I put in the earplugs I bought at the gift shop with the intention of having complete silence. Wrong!

Just for your information, earplugs don't shut out the high pitched voices of 25-year-olds. After a few minutes of frustration, I decided to throw the earplugs away and silently join their joy.

Listen to their joy with me, please:

"Sara, isn't this the best?"

"Yes, I can't believe you took up a collection to bring me here."

"This is your last big fling before you settle into married life. Are you scared?"

"Not really, Jody. Well, maybe a little."

"Should I be scared, Millie? You've been married five years now."

"Sara, I'm not the person you should ask. Things aren't so great right now."

"Hold on, Millie, what are you talking about?"

"Well, the first two years were great. Charles and I did everything together. Then slowly his buddies started hanging around more and more. They all had hockey in common and that seemed fairly harmless to me. I actually encouraged it."

"If you encouraged it, what is the problem?"

"Sara, I did encourage it because they were at our house and they seemed to be having so much fun."

"And?"

"It all happened so slowly. First, it was let's meet at the sports bar for an hour on Friday after work to watch whatever is playing on TV."

"There must be more to the story than that, Millie."

"Yes. Then the hour became all evening. Then they decided they should plan a golf weekend, somewhere warm."

"That doesn't sound so bad."

"Let me finish, Jody."

"Then the boys started a poker night. That led to a skidoo week."

"Oh dear!"

"Now we hardly talk. His life revolves around the boys."

"Why don't you talk about it, Millie? I'm sure Charles would understand."

"When I tried that, Charlotte, he laughed at me. He told me I was being jealous, controlling and selfish. That hurt so much."

"Well, I'm sure he helps you look after the children."

"He's too busy with work, the boys, and sports. I can hardly keep up. It's as if I'm trying to be supermom, super-wife, super-employee, and super-friend. It's too many supers for me."

"How do you feel when you are alone at the end of the day?"

"To be honest, I feel as if I'm buried alive. I'm sad, alone, and I feel as if I've been abandoned."

"Oh! Millie. This is terrible. I had no idea."

"Jodie, we aren't here to solve my problems. We are here to celebrate Sara's journey from single to married life."

"Millie, I feel awful for you. You deserve better."

"Do I, Jodie?"

"I think you do."

"I have no way to solve it. I'm heart broken and can't show it because of the children. There's nothing you can do. Let's just have a good time. We are best friends and we need to make this the best bridal days ever."

At the end of the conversation, I was exhausted. I could not believe how downtrodden this young woman felt. She had lost her voice. She was in a very dark place.

I wondered what I would say to her if I had the opportunity. This thought consumed me as I entered the mediation room. I decided to find some paper and a pen and write down my thoughts. This energy had to be released; otherwise it would spoil my evening.

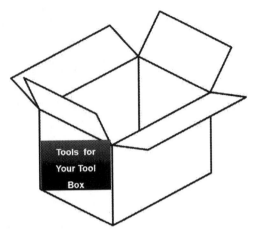

My Suggestions for Millie

Determine your boundaries If we don't have boundaries, other people will impose their expectations on us. These boundaries are essential if we want to ensure our relationships are mutually respectful, supportive and caring. Personal boundaries are measures of our self-esteem. When we set positive personal boundaries, we refrain from becoming co-dependent, dependent, and controlling. We are able to discuss issues calmly and problem solve around any issue.

Know your truth If you do not know your truth, you will always be swayed by others and live life by their rules. We cannot assume that it is going to be better one day. Or that things will be better when…

You only have the present. Accept what "is" and do not rationalize why you shouldn't ask for what you need because you think it is too much or you are being too demanding.

Others will always demand what they want if you are hesitant, inconsistent, or a pushover.

Schedule "Me" Time Just as your partner is scheduling his/her own time and having fun, schedule some special time for yourself. It may be uninterrupted time to sit and read a magazine or book or to have coffee with your friends. Talk to your partner and balance his/her "me" time and your "me" time.

I am not suggesting that you schedule hour for hour. Some weeks you may need more "me" time than your partner does and other times he/she may need more time than you do. It's about the need to honor each person as an individual.

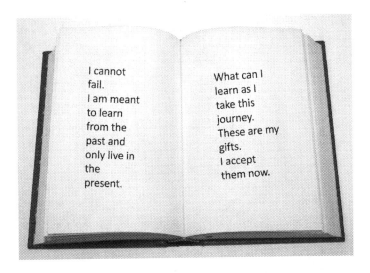

I cannot fail.
I am meant to learn from the past and only live in the present.

What can I learn as I take this journey. These are my gifts. I accept them now.

Chapter 6:   Lessons and Questions to Ponder

Lesson 1:   We need boundaries. It is important to take the time to determine when we need boundaries, with whom we need boundaries, and when expressing our boundaries is essential. Getting angry or agitated after we've agreed to something isn't going to help our relationships.

Question: Do I know my boundaries and am I always honest about them?

Lesson 2:   We all need to know our truths. We need to consider whether or not what we believe is based on our own contemplation of an issue/situation or whether we are blindly accepting the teachings of our parents, teachers, and leaders.

Question: What are my truths, where did they originate, and do I want to keep them or modify them?'

Lesson 3:   Personal time is essential for our physical and mental health. It gives our bodies and minds time to stop, contemplate and restart afresh. It helps us become more productive. Sometimes, it is during those times that we have those "ah ha!" moments. It helps our systems get back on track, making our relationships stronger.

Questions: What do I do to show myself that I am important and that I love myself?
             Do I take time each day to express gratitude?

Today's Gift for Me

I know what it feels like to be buried alive. I also know that I'm the only person who can crawl back up to the surface. If I wait for other people to rescue me, I may never reach the top. I am my own best friend now. I can make myself feel special. I learned that it is not until I love myself that I can truly love others. As a coach once told me, "If I am going through hell, I just keep walking."

There is a Zen Proverb that I read frequently to keep me on the right track.

"Nothing weaker than water. Nothing stronger than rock. Still the slow flow of water can cut through the mountains."

Chapter 7

NEGATIVITY

Today is Day 6 and I am about to have an aromatherapy massage, scalp massage, and hair treatment and styling. What's better than a head-to-toe treatment in a wonderful, loving space?

I was sure that my body was unwinding. The muscles in my neck weren't as tight and my face felt more relaxed. I wasn't clenching my fists or grinding my teeth. That was major progress for me.

Sometimes I feel as if I am the only person in the world who gets uptight. I tried to think of all the possible reasons. My mind seemed to have taken a vacation. My mind was blank. This isn't good, I thought.

I decided to take a pillow and place it on a mat at the foot of my bed. I sat down on the floor, started my meditation music and willed my mind to relax. All I could feel was my body getting tighter and tighter. Not knowing what else to do, I decided to ask myself to list all the negative situations in my life.

First, I remembered an incident when I was about five years old. My mother helped me dress to go outside. I was objecting because I didn't want to go outside alone. She shooed me out and closed the door. I tried to play alone for a while but I was very unhappy. When I thought enough time had passed, I went to the door only to find that I was locked out. A shiver went down my spine. I was abandoned. The devastation was more than I could handle. All I could think was, "Why does my mom hate me so much?"

The sadness that came over me as I remembered that incident was overwhelming. I couldn't believe I have held negative energy related to that incident all these years. I began deep breathing and paying attention only to my breath until I regained my composure.

The second memory related to the death of my father. I was 11 at that time. I remember faking crying. I literally didn't feel anything. My mother sent me to a neighbor's house when it happened. I hated that. Why would anyone send their child away? What a horrible thing to do. Then I remembered returning to our home where my father was waking. I was expected to stand on a stool and kiss his head before the casket was closed. I remembered my body freezing as I heard that request. The request wasn't a question; it was a command. His face was cold to my lips. It felt awful but no one cared about my feelings. As I stepped down from the stool, I noticed this awful smell. I thought it was the Easter Lilies that were in the room. For years after this happened I couldn't go to church at Easter because the sight of Easter Lilies made my body freeze. It was only years later that I discovered that the smell was not Easter Lilies but the smell of wicker furniture.

At this point, all I could do was sit and scan my body to see where the feelings were hidden. I felt alone and sad. I felt invisible, and as if no one really cared about how I felt or how I was coping with this situation.

After about twenty minutes, my mind moved to another incident. When I was 12, we moved to a new city. My mother was going to work in a store to help her friend who was critically ill. I was alone. My mother worked all day. In truth, it seemed as if she worked 24 hours a day, which I know was not the case. I felt like an orphan. She never talked to me or wondered how I was doing. One day in desperation, I went into the store and stole a chocolate bar. A store clerk was standing next to me when I did it. She immediately told my mother and I was severely scolded. I never did get the attention I wanted. I would go to my room, which I shared with my mother, and wished I would die. I couldn't figure out why I couldn't just close my eyes and die. The silence in my room was deafening. Nothing was worth living for, or so I thought at that time.

All of a sudden I realized a common theme. I felt alone and unwanted from birth. I never ever heard anyone say, "I love you." I didn't feel part of my family and always thought that I must have been adopted. I just wanted to leave this earth and find a better place.

Slowly, I sauntered to the spa for my treatment. I needed it at this point. These memories were not helping me relax and enjoy my stay. The negativity was not what I wanted to feel or carry with me from day to day. Then I wondered if others carry negative experiences from their childhood.

The treatments were wonderful. I felt much better after them. They were just what I needed. I decided to sit on my bed and let my mind roam.

I drew a picture of half of an avocado on a sheet of paper. I visualized my real self as the seed in the center. Then I realized that my brain wasn't fully grown until my mid to late 20s. This meant that there was a part of me that was like the flesh of the avocado. It was full of beliefs, feelings, and ideas that were not my own. They belonged to my parents, siblings, friends, teachers, clergy, and other leaders. Finally, I realized that the skin of the avocado was a façade that was keeping my real-self trapped inside.

I needed to follow a process, but what was that method? Slowly, ideas started to enter my consciousness:

1. listen to my internal dialogue,
2. note my beliefs,
3. determine the origin of those beliefs,
4. analyze whether they were serving me well, and
5. if not, change them.

My energy felt low at this point. When that happens I always check to see where I am gazing. Usually, it is downward. At this point I stood up and put my hands in the air as if I just won a jackpot and shifted my gaze to where the wall met the ceiling. I bounced up and down and held that pose for one minute. Next, I decided to do exercises I learned a few years ago. The first I called the Belly Button and Third Eye exercise.

I placed the middle finger of my right hand in my belly button and the middle finger of my left hand on my third eye (it's in a hollow between our eyebrows) and pulled upward as I took six deep breaths in through my nose and out through my mouth.

Next, I did several energy exercises I learned during a Brain Gym course to ensure that I was open and connected to universal wisdom.

I felt much better when I finished my routine and decided to sit down to sip on lemon water and listen to a recording of big band music. I needed this to keep my spirits up and let the feeling of peace settle into my body and mind.

My childhood is over. The memories serve no purpose unless I learn from them and move on.

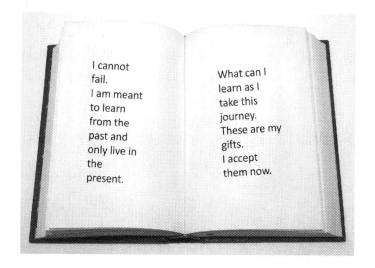

I cannot fail.
I am meant to learn from the past and only live in the present.

What can I learn as I take this journey.
These are my gifts.
I accept them now.

Chapter 7:   **Lessons and Questions to Ponder**

Lesson 1:   The things we think we've forgotten may be lying dormant or buried in our bodies and psyche. The unfortunate thing about past memories is that they may not be accurate. Accurate or not, they can affect how we feel in the present. Therefore, it is essential to get in touch with and release old energy that is not serving any useful purpose.

Questions: How many negative memories am I harbouring and am I willing and able to release them?

If I cannot release them on my own, am I willing to seek professional help?

Lesson 2:   Negative memories can be coloring the lens through which we observe and interpret our world. Therefore, it is up to each of us to understand how our past is affecting how we interpret events and react to them. We have only three options: fight, flight or relax.

Questions: Am I able to relax and deal with all circumstances or do I automatically go into fight or flight mode?

Am I willing to learn the skills to relax?

Lesson 3:   Negativity affects our mental and physical health. Positive thoughts and emotions are essential to our well-being.

Question: Am I willing to pay attention to my thoughts, note those that are negative, and reframe them?

Today's Gift for Me

I have a choice 100 per cent of the time. I can see circumstances through a negative or a positive lens. I have made mistakes. I've learned the lessons. These lessons help me understand others better. I am empathetic and compassionate.

I've learned to be patient, non-judgmental, and open to learning from every situation. When my thoughts become rigid, I pretend I'm a tree. I remember that in a storm the tree bends and accommodates its circumstances. It does not fight what is. As soon as the storm passes, it returns to its rightful posture and continues to grow toward the light.

I can be a light for you and you can be a light for me. As Seth Adam Smith says in Rip Van Winkle and the Pumpkin Lantern, "And so I tell you, restless one, that no matter what happens, when things get dark, look to the light, and keep moving forward in faith."

Chapter 8

THE DARK SIDE

This is my last day at the spa. I feel exhilarated and exhausted at the same time. Even though I've learned so much about myself, I still feel as if I'm meeting myself for the first time. I needed this full relaxation body massage. I'd been ruminating about what I would choose as my optional service. Finally, I decided that I'd get my hair styled and fingernails manicured. Then I'd be ready for my journey home.

At the spa, I met Jean and Edith. They were preparing for their massages. Neither of them looked very happy. I noticed how Jean held her arms close to her body. Her lips were turned down and her eyes were as cold as ice.

Edith was joking but her voice was loud and firm, and it had a very cutting tone. She seemed to be laughing at her own jokes. The humor appeared to be a form of gossip and belittling of others.

All of a sudden, I realized I was judging them. That wasn't my intent, but nevertheless that was exactly what I was doing. I tiptoed to my table area and moved the screen to provide maximum privacy. I slipped out of my smock and under the sheet on the massage table.

Jojo, or that's what she said her name was, introduced herself and began my full body massage. All I could think was that this was my last chance to relax before heading home. In the meantime, Edith and Jean had no intention of being quiet. I'd gotten used to the chatter and I decided just to rest and listen.

"Edith, isn't Maria's new hairdo horrible?"

"I know. She looks like a hippo."

"Whoever told her it was nice anyway?"

"Not me."

"And did you see what Mary did to her kitchen?"

"I did. It's a disaster. Who puts bright yellow in a kitchen these days? All you have to do is pick up a fashion magazine to know it is out of style."

"She said she didn't need an interior decorator to help her because she knew exactly what she wanted done."

"Well, her tastes are terrible."

"Did you know that Bernie bought a new car?"

"She did that to outdo Audrey."

"The two of them are always competing. When Audrey gets something new, Bernie will immediately want something better."

"I'd never compete with anyone, would you?"

"Nah. It's not worth it."

"Jean, did you know that Monica is going out with John."

"No, Edith! Philip has only been dead eight months."

"I know. No respect. She probably couldn't wait for him to pass so that she could meet someone new."

"Sure, Evelyn's daughter is getting a divorce."

"What?"

"They had such an expensive wedding last year. I heard it cost their parents $40,000.00."

"They put on quite a show didn't they? What a waste of money. They would have been better off giving them money towards a house."

"I know. You wouldn't know but they were royalty."

"This will teach them."

"And rightly so."

"Did you know that David lost his job three months ago and Julie is prancing around as if he's still a manager with his firm?"

"Go on! She's lost touch with reality then. She needs to get a grip and he needs to find a new job."

"He's probably looking for something that pays the same salary."

"Good luck with that."

"Did you know that Joanne has decided to have a baby?"

"Isn't she single?"

"That doesn't stop women these days."

"She'll soon learn that it isn't that easy to raise a child on your own."

"She'll get what she deserves, now won't she."

"I'm so happy you and I don't have any problems, aren't you?

"For sure. We are the only two sane ones in our group."

"I know. I know."

As I climbed down from the table, Jojo shook her head from side to side and rolled her eyes as if to say, "What dorks." She handed me my water, told me to drink lots of it, and left as quietly as she arrived.

I sat in a lounging chair pondering this conversation. What did it mean? How could two people feel so self-righteous and simultaneously see all their friends as losers? I wondered what I would say if I was part of that conversation. I did have a few ideas and I reached for my journal and started to write.

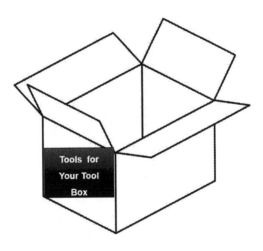

Tools for
Your Tool
Box

For Jean and Edith

Pivot

Pivoting is a tool I use to look at situations from a variety of perspectives. If I am being negative or overly optimistic, I will either write the situation from its opposite perspective or from the perspective of a neutral person who is looking in on the situation.

Hidden Self

We have a picture of the self we want others to see. In truth, there is a part of us we try and hide from others. For example, we think we are too shy, too bold, too tall, too short, too young or too old. I know now that if I am feeling negative about something, it might mean that there is a lesson I need to learn. It may relate to an unresolved issue, a limiting belief, or a behavior I don't even know I display. When I uncover the real reason for my reactions, I can determine what options I have to solve the issue, change my belief, or modify my behavior. I'm always gentle with myself, or at least I try to be compassionate.

Vision

Visioning means thinking about all aspect of our life and our personality, defining our core values and writing a script, which contains sight, sound and feelings of who and what I want to be to others and to myself.

As those thoughts subsided, it was time to see if there were lessons I needed to learn from this encounter.

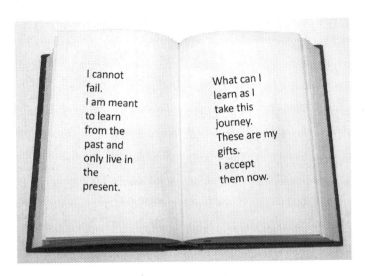

I cannot fail. I am meant to learn from the past and only live in the present.

What can I learn as I take this journey. These are my gifts. I accept them now.

Chapter 8:   Lessons and Questions to Ponder

Lesson 1:   Life is a journey. It is important to focus our attention on the inside rather than on the outside. That's easier said than done. It is essential for our growth, mentally and spiritually.

Question: Am I busy watching and judging others or am I focusing on my own growth and how I can be of service to others?

Lesson 2: Most things in the universe have opposites. Black and white, happy and sad, anger and calm are just a few illustrations. For example, both happiness and sadness are based on fear. If I only want to be happy, I will become sad or frustrated when any circumstance attempts to disrupt that feeling. The point of poise is in the center – neither happy nor sad. I don't need to run from sadness or focus on only being happy. I can just let situations and people be. What is just is. There is no need for me to act as judge and jury.

Question: What do I notice most? What circumstances bring out the shadow side of me? Do I know… really know?

Lesson 3: The intention of life is to grow and create a greater connection with our true selves. That takes time and patience; maybe even a whole lifetime. Therefore, it is essential to know that we were made in God's image. We are all perfect at the core. Our job is to connect to that core, live through that lens, and leave the world a better place than we found it.

Question: How far am I from my core and what am I doing to connect to it on a daily or weekly basis?

Today's Gift for Me

Many aspects of life are paradoxes. Everything has an opposite. I try to realize when I become attached or addicted to one pole or the other. For example, if I become agitated when happy situations end, I know that I am attached to happiness. I need sadness too. The sadness helps improve my memory for certain events, and it causes me to stop and really think about a situation before I act. It improves my desire to change my situation and take beneficial action.

I know that emotions are just information. I feel them without judgement and search for the message.

Chapter 9

THE JOURNEY HOME

Now, as I leave, I realize I needed this time away. I climbed in the taxi and asked to be taken to the airport. Silently as I watched the sights and listened to the sounds, I realized what a privilege it is to see and hear clearly. My thoughts drifted and before I knew it I was at the airport. Pulling my bags, I checked in and began to visualize my arrival at home. My thoughts were disturbed when I heard my name being called.

"Hi, I'm Aimee. Do you remember me? From the Spa, I mean."

"Yes Aimee, I do."

"You seemed so distant. We never did get to speak."

"I was on a silent retreat."

"I came to relax but all I did was rehash old history."

"Yes. I heard."

"You know, I feel so badly about myself, consequently I feel alone."

"What seems to be bothering you, Aimee?"

"I work and come home, cook and lie on the couch. I have no purpose. No meaningful relationships. Life is boring and time is long."

"Do you have any goals for your life, Aimee?"

"No. I walk my dogs. Well, in truth I don't really walk them. I'm too tired after dinner to do that."

"What would you like for your life?"

"I want a purpose. I want to feel needed. I want to belong."

"Could you set one thing to do each day rather than lying on the couch each evening, Aimee?"

"Like what? I wouldn't know where to begin. Any ideas?"

"Could you make a schedule for yourself? Maybe before dinner two days a week you could walk your dogs for 30 minutes. Another day you could commit to call a friend or family member to see how they are doing. Maybe another day you could consider doing a good deed for someone else or going to the library or take a class. Those are just some ideas. What excites you, Aimee?

"I like to quilt. I like it when my daughter or son invites me for Saturday brunch. I like to read. I love getting a massage or my hair done at a salon."

"Could you promise to do something you love once a month? Something special for yourself, I mean."

"That's selfish isn't it?"

"Not really, Aimee, if we don't love ourselves with all our warts, it is difficult to love others with all their flaws. I think we will always be lonely if we do not become our own best friends."

"I never thought of it that way. I always thought of people who pampered themselves as being self-centered and childish."

"This is a solo journey. Each person moves forward at his or her own pace. That may annoy us but it is the way life is structured."

"I feel as if I should be punished for something."

"I don't know your belief system but I do believe that God does not judge. The universe accepts us as we are. What we call mistakes are lessons. We take from them and keep moving forward. That's my thinking, Aimee"

"I always thought I was going to hell for all my misdeeds."

"Where did you get that belief, Aimee?"

"From my parents."

"You are here to learn, grow and evolve. Not to be punished and rejected. You are perfect as you are."

"I don't see how you can say that. I've never fit in."

"You will not fit in everywhere or with everyone."

"But sometimes I feel like a real outsider."

"You will until you find your group."

"What do you mean by my group?"

"I mean people who are on a journey. People who are not interested in judging and criticizing you. People who respect the fact that you will fall many times and will support you as you pick yourself up and move forward."

"Do they exist?"

"I believe that when we judge others we are really judging ourselves and focusing on our weaknesses. That is easy and not helpful. It is better to focus on our strengths, use them to overcome our weaknesses, and assist others to do the same. Aimee, our worlds are a direct reflection of our true thoughts and beliefs. First, we have to change ourselves. Then our worlds will respond automatically. Respond for the better, I mean."

"Do you really believe that my world is a direct reflection of my thoughts and beliefs?"

"Aimee, I really do. We need to change our thoughts and beliefs to change our lives."

"This is new information for me."

"That's okay, Aimee, it took me some time to realize that what I was seeing and experiencing I was creating. Please don't take my word for it. Think about it and decide for yourself."

"Whoops, that's my flight they're calling. Nice talking to you mystery woman."

Now I really need to go home. I came to relax and rejuvenate. I found the lessons I needed to learn. This was the perfect situation. I couldn't run away from the lessons. I may not have all the answers but my life will never be the same.

These seven days at the spa have taught me to be patient with myself, love myself as I am, serve others, and keep searching for my true self.

I have made many mistakes, been judgmental and overbearing. I tried to fix everyone because I didn't want them to go through difficult situations. The truth is that we cannot help another person until that person genuinely wants the help.

My intentions are honorable but others may not receive my words or actions as I intend them.

I realize that I have the perfect husband, the perfect job and the perfect children. They are in my life because there are lessons I needed to learn.

I'm happy. Not perfect, just happy. I have more tools in my tool box than I realized. My life isn't as mixed up as I thought. My gratitude list is growing steadily.

As I twirl around, I felt like a million dollars. My arms just swung freely. I am in heaven. I have everything I need and more.

The ladies at the spa acted as mirrors for my other thoughts and hang-ups. I owe them. Each lady was a gift. Without her story, I wouldn't have realized what a privileged life I live.

I walked to the Thai Air desk to check in and I felt that I looked 10 years younger. I grinned like a Cheshire cat. There was a spring in my step.

I realized I didn't come to the spa to learn these lessons but I needed the lessons more than I needed the silence or the massages.

Today is the first day of the rest of my life. I choose to focus on the lessons I've learned rather than on the memories behind the lessons.

I am remarkable! (May sound self-centered but it is true). You are remarkable. Please look in your tool box, take an inventory of all the wonderful knowledge and skills you have learned over the years. Use them all to your advantage.

We only have one opportunity to make this journey. Let's walk it together and support each other along the way.

Until we meet in person, may the Universe Bless You Always.

About the Author

Brenda Kelleher-Flight is a coach who believes in each person's right to a happy fulfilling life.

She's learned that many of us experience similar situations, yet we feel alone and unhappy. She believes that we are not alone; each person is on a journey. The only goal is to befriend oneself and keep moving toward the light.

Brenda has many tools which can be utilized along the way. As you spend time at this spa with her at the spa take time to find the tools that serve you best and use them freely.

Read more of Brenda's work at *www.gdpconsulting.ca*